Leicestershire & Rutland

A PORTRAIT IN COLOUR

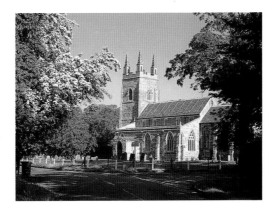

BILL MEADOWS & BRYAN WAITES

COUNTRYSIDE BOOKS

Other counties in this series include:

BUCKINGHAMSHIRE	ESSEX
CHESHIRE	HAMPSHIRE
DERBYSHIRE	SUFFOLK
DEVON	SURREY
DORSET	SUSSEX

First published 1997
© Photographs, Bill Meadows 1997
© Text, Bryan Waites 1997

COUNTRYSIDE BOOKS
3 CATHERINE ROAD
NEWBURY, BERKSHIRE

ISBN 1 85306 474 2

The photograph on page 1 is of Stanford on Avon church

Designed by Mon Mohan
Produced through MRM Associates Ltd, Reading
Printed in Singapore

Contents

INTRODUCTION

Leicestershire is still the unknown county to many people. They may have passed through it on the M1 motorway but it remains to them anonymous, and shrouded in a regional image largely created by writers such as Hilaire Belloc.

Better-informed people would at least know some of our popular claims to fame: Red Leicester and the 'king of cheeses', Stilton; Melton pork pies and hunt cake; Ruddles County Ale from Rutland. They would be aware of the renowned Leicester market; the well-known fox-hunts such as the Quorn and the Cottesmore; legends about 'painting the town red' at Melton, and the famous horseshoes which have hung for centuries in Oakham Castle. They would have heard of England's largest man-made lake, Rutland Water; of the battlefield of Bosworth and the fairytale Belvoir Castle, location for the films *Little Lord Fauntleroy* and *Hazard of Hearts*. Others would have visited our 'Little Switzerland' as Charnwood Forest, where a schoolboy found the oldest fossil in the world, has been called.

So the list goes on. This 'anonymous' county has many other remarkable features: the 'Ivanhoe Country' of Ashby-de-la-Zouch; famous writers such as C. P. Snow, Joe Orton and Colin Wilson; the Attenboroughs; the Haymarket Theatre with its world premières of shows like *Me and My Girl*; the TV chimps from Twycross Zoo; and the acclaimed libraries and museums.

Leicestershire can claim many 'firsts': the first BBC local radio station; the first traffic wardens; the first town guides; the first environmental town trail in 1972; the first 'park and ride' scheme. Recently Leicester has been designated Britain's first Environmental City. It was honoured at the Earth Summit at Rio de Janeiro in 1992, and in 1996 received the European Sustainable City Award for its environmental campaigns – the only city in Britain to do so. No wonder people say that Leicestershire and Leicester are undergoing a cultural and economic renaissance.

All this is well supported by multiracial harmony in an area which has a rich diversity of Europeans, Asians, Africans, West Indians and others speaking a wide range of languages. Leicester itself has become more exotic and exciting. It has bright lights and festivals like the Navratri, Dashera and Diwali celebrations in October and November each year – the biggest Hindu festival in the western world. There are gourmet restaurants all over the city representing most of the world's cuisine, and a walk down Belgrave Road is like being transported to far-away Asia.

Leicestershire's attraction, in essence, lies not in spectacular scenery or dramatic features but in subtle beauty and in a man-made landscape which can be enjoyed all the more when it is understood in its historical context. Built, as it might seem, almost to a formula, there sits centrally a great city of approximately 300,000 people. Once, perhaps, a capital of the Coritani tribe, and certainly a significant Roman town, Leicester became an important medieval centre and later an industrial and commercial city with many worldwide links, especially in hosiery, knitwear, footwear and engineering. It was indeed a fine Victorian provincial city. Today, this history can be traced through archaeology, buildings and townscape – but the hidden Leicester has to be discovered.

Around this great city at a distance of no more than 20 miles can be found a satellite collection of market towns illustrating the agricultural heritage of the county. Melton Mowbray, Oakham, Uppingham, Market Harborough, Hinckley, Lutterworth, Market Bosworth, Ashby-de-la-Zouch and Loughborough provide now, as in the past, fine examples of England's vintage market towns which have all the appeal and character, all the range of shopping facilities and attractions, one would expect. Now their populations have been sharply increased by the commuters who live in them and work in the city.

Two recreational areas stand out: Charnwood Forest in Leicestershire and Rutland Water, as from April 1997 in the re-established county of Rutland. They balance each other as the city population seeks refreshment in either an easterly or a westerly direction. The former, an ancient mountain range once covered by desert and once volcanic, rises in craggy formations to more than 900 feet at Bardon Hill. Views across to the Trent valley power stations and towards Lincoln are possible from Old John and Beacon Hill. Bradgate Park, once the home of Lady Jane Grey, still retains the ruins of a great house and deer park, a focal point for tourists at all times of year.

Rutland Water, to the east, is reached by traversing the marlstone escarpment, which finds its crowning glory at Belvoir Castle, overlooking the Vale of Belvoir. Attractive stone villages seem to rise straight from the earth as their ochre-coloured stone reflects the sunlight on a blue-skyed summer's day. Further east, beyond Rutland Water, the famous Clipsham, Ketton and Barnack stones can be seen in the buildings as their character changes. Soon the edge of the Fenland is reached and from Stamford begins the land of John Clare, the Peasant Poet; the black peat; the dykes and the glorious skies. Imagine siting an artificial lake the size of Windermere in England's smallest county! Almost three per cent of Rutland's surface area was used. Despite strong objections at the time, now most people praise Rutland Water as a triumph of the 21st century which arrived ahead of its time. Try to see it as the sun rises or sets over the water. Walk along its pleasant waterside paths or cycle if you prefer. Visit the outstanding nature reserve or take part in the varied watersports available. Rutland Water has enhanced Rutland and it has transformed lives.

Every part of Leicestershire and Rutland rewards exploration, and as this book shows, it is a region of contrasts and pleasing views. The people have left their mark in the wonderful old buildings and communities, and in the stories which have been handed down through the generations. I came to live and work in Leicester in 1961 and moved to Rutland in 1969. This book offers a view into both counties which I hope will allow readers to discover them both in all their brilliant colours.

Bryan Waites

Ashby-de-la-Zouch

To many, north-west Leicestershire is the forgotten corner of the county, which people pass through but may not stop to investigate. Yet it has a powerful appeal derived from its old industries, now largely gone. Additionally, the East Midlands Airport, the famous Donington Park racing circuit and the award-winning Snibston Discovery Park, Coalville, are up-to-date attractions which make the area better known.

Ashby-de-la-Zouch Castle has become famous as the location of the fictional tournament in Sir Walter Scott's *Ivanhoe*, and the area around it is now known as 'Ivanhoe Country'.

The castle was originally a Norman manor house, later converted into a fortress by Lord Hastings in the 15th century. The Hastings tower, built in 1476, was connected to the kitchens by an underground passage. W. G. Hoskins writes that the castle represented 'the last impact of feudalism on the landscape . . . it is neither a true castle nor a country house . . . built in a time of civil war and anarchy . . . it was finished only fifteen years or so before the commencement of the first true country house in Leicestershire and it serves as a sort of prelude to the new civilisation that was to arise from the ruins of feudalism'. During the Civil War the castle was occupied by Royalists, who were besieged for over a year until they surrendered in 1646. Afterwards the castle was partly destroyed, but it is now in the care of English Heritage.

Ashby-de-la-Zouch is the historic market town of the region and in the 19th century was described as 'not a manufacturing town . . . but genteel and respectable'. Its main street retains an imposing aura and some fine buildings with several interesting passageways.

Ashby's prominence grew when nearby Moira failed as a spa town. Mineral water discovered during mining operations at Bath Colliery near Moira was taken to Ashby and in 1822 the Ivanhoe Baths were built, followed by the Royal Hotel in 1826. By 1846 *White's Directory* reported that Ashby was 'a handsome and highly salubrious market town and watering place'.

Moira Furnace (*inset*) is an impressive 19th-century blast furnace, perhaps the best preserved in Europe. It was built about 1804 by the Earl of Moira to exploit the mineral wealth of the Ashby Woulds, nearby. It was the forerunner of larger, more advanced furnaces and the complex includes lime kilns, casting shed, engine house and museum. The former Ashby Canal, which brought raw materials to the furnace, is close by.

Staunton Harold Hall

Just on the border between Leicestershire and Derbyshire there is a remarkable concentration of historic buildings, all within 5 miles of each other. Calke Abbey is the baroque mansion (1701–3) where it is said 'time stood still' because the reclusive owner, Sir Vauncey Harpur Crewe left the house virtually unchanged. Melbourne Hall was the early 17th-century home of Lord Melbourne, the Victorian prime minister; Breedon on the Hill church stands on a 180-foot limestone knoll and is the site of an Iron Age fort and Saxon abbey; Staunton Harold Hall and church, perhaps the most splendid of all these monuments, were described by Sir Nikolaus Pevsner as 'unsurpassed in the country, certainly as far as Englishness is concerned'.

The view from the parkland at Staunton Harold, looking over the lake towards Holy Trinity church in the foreground with the Palladian-style Hall beyond, is one of the most entrancing you will find anywhere.

Once there was a village too, but this was removed in the 14th century in favour of sheep ranching. The Shirley family held the manor for over five centuries. In the early 17th century Sir Henry Shirley had a mansion built at the centre of the 1,700-acre parish. Large deer parks were converted into farmland in 1623. The present Hall was designed and built by Washington, 5th Earl Ferrers (1760–78), but not quite finished at his death. The formal gardens of the late 17th century were mostly swept away by the same earl, who replaced them with the more 'natural'

scenery we see today. The Hall narrowly escaped demolition in the 1950s, and was sold in 1954. It is now a Sue Ryder Home.

Holy Trinity church was one of the few churches built during the troubled times of the Commonwealth. It was begun by Sir Robert Shirley, an ardent Royalist, in 1653, as an act of piety and defiance 'when all things sacred were throughout the Nation either demolisht or profaned'. It was not completed until 1665. The original cushions, hangings, panelling and painted ceiling remain and there is a wrought-iron screen by Robert Bakewell.

Many monuments to the Shirley family are to be found in nearby Breedon church. There is also a memorial to John Johnson, the 'esteem'd and faithful servant' of Laurence Shirley, 4th Earl Ferrers. John suffered an 'untimely death'. The monument does not record that it was the Earl who murdered John, in 1760. Sentenced to hang at Tyburn after trial by his peers at Westminster, Laurence Shirley asked to be beheaded at the Tower, but his request was refused. He travelled in style, richly dressed, to his execution in his own landau, and was given the privilege of being hanged by a silken cord instead of the hangman's rope. Not only was he the first man to die on the 'new drop', but he was also the last peer of the realm to be hanged. His remains were believed to have been brought back to Staunton Harold.

Old John and Bradgate Park

Charnwood Forest is not all forest but a mixture of bracken-covered hills with craggy, dramatic rock outcrops, farmland, woodland, reservoirs, quarries, villages, deer parks and the M1 motorway running through the middle. For many years it has been the lungs of Leicester, providing vintage countryside for citizens living only 7 miles away: they can be on top of Old John from the city centre within half an hour.

What a view they have! The Old John Tower stands nearly 700 feet above sea level and provides a panorama over all east Leicestershire, as well as views of the city and more distant vistas. Millions of years ago the area was the site of a series of volcanic cones even now detectable in the sharp, angled rock outcrops. This has made Charnwood an alien area within the serene Midland landscapes around it; so much so that it has been likened to a miniature Wales or even a 'Little Switzerland'. After the volcanic action the area became a desert and clues to its past, such as fossil wadis, can still be found. The rich geology has encouraged industry and quarrying and made Mountsorrel granite famous as a building and road stone.

The Old John Tower was built about 1786 and has been called a folly as well as a hunting tower. A local story explains that it was erected to commemorate an old retainer of the Greys of Bradgate Park who was killed by a falling maypole during a party.

Below Old John the river Lin traverses a tiny gorge, then opens out into a wider valley. Here is Bradgate Park and the ruin which was once the home of Lady Jane Grey, the nine-day Queen of England (*inset*). Bradgate was enclosed from the wasteland to form a deer park before 1247 and it still retains that original appearance. It was part of the manor of Groby and owned by the Ferrers family. When Sir Edward de Grey was created Lord Ferrers in 1445 the estate passed into the line of this influential family.

Bradgate House was begun in 1490 and completed about 1510. It was one of the first unfortified brick-built country houses in England. Perhaps at about this time the villagers of Bradgate were removed outside the park to the 'new town at Lin ford', now known as Newtown Linford.

The Greys, created Earls of Stamford in 1628, continued to live in the house until the 1740s when it became neglected, and finally ruinous. It was purchased in 1928 by Charles Bennion, who made it over to the city and county of Leicester. It was designated a country park in 1970 and the whole estate of more than 1,254 acres is managed by Bradgate Park Trust.

Bosworth Field 1485

Each year, on 22nd August, an insertion appears in the *Leicester Mercury*:

ROLL OF HONOUR

PLANTAGENET. Richard. King, Soldier, Statesman. Died fighting bravely at the battle of Bosworth. Deeply loved and still mourned by North Country Britons. IN MEMORIAM.

The wording may vary year by year but its sentiments remain the same: it commemorates the death of Richard III at the battle of Bosworth in Leicestershire in 1485. In Leicester Cathedral you can find a splendid memorial stone to King Richard on the chancel floor. Until vandalized, his statue stood in Castle Gardens, Leicester, but it has been resited near to Bow Bridge (*inset*), where his body was thrown into the river Soar after the defeat.

Bosworth is of national importance because it marked the end of the Middle Ages and the end of the War of the Roses. Richard was the last of the Plantagenets and the victor, Henry, the first Tudor. Today, you can visit the battlefield and, surrounded by flying banners, relive it all. You can pause inside Sutton Cheney church where Richard prayed before the battle. Go to the Battlefield Centre to see replica shields, armour, a model battle scene, flags, and slide and film shows to help you understand the battle. You can follow a Battlefield Trail where information boards display the events of 1485 and above fly huge flags – Henry's red dragon and Richard's white boar. You will find the spring where Richard drank before the battle – King Dick's Well – and the memorial stone in King Richard's Field, where he died.

Leicester Market

Leicester market, with all its vigour, vitality and visual appeal, is the real heart of the city. It is the spirit of the place, and its characters and cosmopolitan composition are 'a sight not to be missed by anyone who visits the city'.

One of Britain's largest open-air markets, it is situated right in the shopping centre, next to the Town Hall Square and with many attractive medieval lanes nearby. Once, the town walls followed Horse Fair Lane and Gallowtree Gate, and the Saturday market was established in 1298 in the corner between the walls. Nearby were other markets: in the present High Street – swinemarket; in Silver Street – sheepmarket, and at High Cross a Wednesday market for country produce. In 1977 the former High Cross pillar was re-erected in Cheapside near an entrance to the present retail market, a fitting harmonisation of history and modern development.

In 1972–5 a brick-built market centre was erected which now occupies part of the market place. The fascinating cast-iron Victorian fish market (1881) is definitely worth a visit. The Saturday market was also a cattle market from the 1300s to the 1500s and from 1797 to 1804. In that year it moved next door into Horsefair Leys, now Town Hall Square. Here the cattle market stayed until it moved to the purpose-built Aylestone Road market in 1872. Once the cattle market moved, the way was open to build a new town hall to replace the Guildhall. As a result of a competition, F. J. Hames's design was accepted and built between 1873 and 1876.

Town Hall Square itself is a pleasant oasis in the busy city, with its interesting fountain (*inset*), also designed by F. J. Hames, its trees and floral displays.

The Diwali Festival of Light

Leicester is one of Britain's foremost multicultural centres, with people from all parts of Europe, the West Indies, India, Pakistan, Bangladesh, and many other countries. During the past 20 years this has added a cosmopolitan aspect to Leicester – from sari shops down Belgrave Road to a multitude of restaurants, colourful festivals and temples – which has given a new zest and variety to city life.

The Jain temple in Oxford Street (*inset*) stands on the site of a former church. Leicester's 1,000-strong Jain community bought the premises in 1979 and turned it into a place of pilgrimage for Jains all over the world, as it is the only temple to represent the religion's different sects. Consecrated images were shipped from India in 1985, and the official opening ceremony was held in 1988. The finest examples of traditional Indian architecture in the western world are to be found here – hand carved pillars, ornate domes and ceilings in sandstone, shrines of white marble, stained glass and mirrored mosaics. In 1996 the prime minister visited this unique Jain centre and praised the tolerance of the Jain religion, the craftsmanship displayed, and the contribution made to Britain by the Asian community.

The biggest Hindu festival in the world occurs in Leicester in October and November each year. Thousands enjoy the Navratri and Dashera festival – literally 'festival of nine nights' – celebrating the victory of good Lord Rama over the evil King Ravana. A 30-foot effigy of the ten-headed Ravana is burnt.

There follows the Diwali Festival of Light, the most important date in the Hindu calendar, marking the start of the new year. More than 6,000 lamps line Belgrave Road and the lights are switched on by the lord mayor. Street entertainments include music and dancing, and fireworks illuminate the sky as 50,000 people throng Belgrave Road and Cossington Street. Many come from all parts of Britain, and others fly in from all over the world specially for the event.

The City of Leicester

The clock tower, built in 1868, has become a symbol of Leicester. It represented a new kind of structure – perhaps the first traffic island in Britain – and it was the sign of Leicester's business and commercial prosperity in Victorian times. It established itself 'in not a few hearts as the hub of the universe', so said F. E. Skillington in *The Plain Man's History of Leicester*.

It was built by the well-known architect Joseph Goddard, 'proudly bristling with canopies and wavy with crockets'. Spiral mouldings around the square shaft indicated the inside staircase. Below there are four statues: Simon de Montfort, William Wyggeston, Sir Thomas

White and Alderman Gabriel Newton – all Leicester worthies. Some felt that 'it will long stand as a significant record of the talent and artistic ability of the Architect, contractor and sculptor'. Others declared: 'it pretends to be the centre . . . it is too foolishly insignificant' and, 'it is a piece of ripe mid-Victorian Gothic; dignified, well-proportioned and as thickly encrusted with ornament as a child's birthday cake'.

The buildings of the University of Leicester (*inset*), set on rising ground 1 mile south of the clock tower are a fitting symbol of modern Leicester. A University College was founded in 1926 in the county lunatic asylum, later called the Fielding Johnson building ('almost Prussian, a big symmetrical block of stock brick'). When university status was granted in 1957, with over 1,000 students, a serious building programme had to be undertaken.

The Engineering building by James Stirling and James Gowan (1959–63) created a stir with its 'complex geometry with oblique angles'. Then came the Charles Wilson building by Denys Lasdun and Partners (1962–7) for the students' union, with 'exposed concrete . . . stressed horizontals and contrasting chimney-like service tower', all jutting out in unequal parts. The Attenborough building by Ove Arup Associates (1968–70) was the tallest tower of all and was named to commemorate a former principal, F. L. Attenborough, father of Richard and David. There are 18 storeys 'prickly with window units angled out from top to bottom'.

In a generally low-profile city, it is the university buildings, the new symbol of academic, vocational futures, which make the skyline appropriately controversial.

Victoria Park

In 1785 Queen's Walk, now New Walk, was laid out as a traffic-free promenade. People could walk from the city centre for ¾ mile along this unique pedestrian way to the new race course. By 1823 the latter had been replaced by Victoria Park. County cricket, soccer and rugby were played in the park and it is still the scene of various sports.

Dominating the park today is the war memorial by Sir Edwin Lutyens; built in 1923, it now commemorates the dead of two world wars. It is in Portland stone and, in 1925, Lutyens designed a smaller replica for New Delhi, India. The processional way and formal gardens add grandeur to its setting. Two gate lodges in the park were also designed by Lutyens in the early 1930s.

Nearby is De Montfort Hall, Leicester's premier concert hall, built in 1913. Until this was erected, Leicester lacked a large assembly hall, the only one available being the Temperance Hall in Granby Street owned by Thomas Cook, which was of limited value because of the ban on alcohol.

Matters were brought to a head in 1907 when the British Association for the Advancement of Science met in Leicester; the members had to be accommodated in a loggia constructed around the lawn of Museum Square, New Walk. The addition of flowers and an orchestra helped to make this venue a surprising success and the seeds for a more permanent structure were sown.

Despite complaints that Victoria Park was too distant from the city centre, plans were formulated and a competition was held to find the best design. It was won by the designer of the Usher Hall, Edinburgh, Shirley Harrison. The cost was £21,000 and the hall held seating for 3,000, all with an unobstructed view. Alfred Corah, of the famous hosiery and knitwear firm, gave the great organ as a personal gift and he was the first to play it when he gave a recital to his employees in 1914.

The hall is impressive in its purity of design. It is in rendered brick with wide pedimental gables and a Tuscan colonnade. It is built on brick piers because of soft subsoil, and it is thought that this may be one of the reasons for its

excellent acoustics, which have been much praised from all quarters; many believe it to be the finest concert hall in the Midlands. A variety of entertainments is provided throughout the year.

Victoria Park is home to Leicester University, De Montfort Hall, the war memorial, and Wyggeston & Queen Elizabeth I College, with the church of St James the Greater just across the road; as such, it is starting to develop into the cultural centre of Leicester.

Bells and Loughborough

During the 19th century Loughborough became an important industrial centre, mainly because of its central position, its railways and canals, and its good water and power supplies. With so many large centres of population within 50 miles, it was well situated to market its products.

Lace and hosiery were a staple industry. Then, towards the end of the century, came Brush Electrical Engineering Co., producing dynamos, arc lamps, street lights and eventually locomotives, buses and trams. In 1884 Herbert Morris Crane Works were established and later chemical and scientific industries such as Fisons Pharmaceuticals. Educational provision blossomed so that as well as many schools and colleges Loughborough now has a university.

Although Loughborough is famous for many things, one of the most outstanding is its bell industry. John Taylor & Co Bellfounders arrived in Loughborough in 1839 – to recast the bells of All Saints. They thrived, at first in Packhorse Lane and later, as the business prospered from 1860, in Cherry Orchard near Freehold Street.

In 1881 the firm cast 'Great Paul' for St Paul's, London. This was the largest bell to be cast by bellfounders in Britain and weighed over 16 tons. By 1892 Taylor's was the world's largest bell foundry.

Taylor's have supplied bells for churches, cathedrals, town halls and public buildings all over the world and it has been written that 'it is almost impossible for a person to stand in any part of England on a Sunday from which the ringing of bells made by Messrs John Taylor & Co. cannot be heard ...' This may be wishful thinking in an age when there are fewer churches, fewer services and more noise on Sundays than ever before, but we should still remember the way bells figure in our lives at weddings, funerals, celebrations, as signals or warnings, and especially every day when they chime the time.

Some also play a tune, as do the 47 bells in the famous Carillon Tower in Queen's Park, Loughborough (*inset*). This first grand carillon in Britain was built of local bricks and it is a war memorial and museum of the armed forces. It was dedicated on 22nd July, 1923. There are wonderful views of Charnwood Forest from the top of the tower and recitals are played on the bells at certain times during the year. The Carillon Tower has become Loughborough's landmark and symbol.

The Great Central Railway

The Great Central Railway completed its 'London extension' from Nottingham to Aylesbury in 1899. The Beeching axe fell on this railway on 5th September 1966, when it ceased to be a through route; the last train on any part of the line ran on 3rd May 1969.

In 1973 a group of enthusiasts formed Main Line Steam Trust Ltd, which became the Great Central Railway Co in 1976 and managed to purchase part of the line. Now, after years of great effort, the company has restored the line from Leicester North (Belgrave and Birstall) through to Rothley, Quorn and Woodhouse into Loughborough Central station. This is attractive country on the edge of Charnwood and it is a true delight to see steam trains once again running through it.

All this is reminiscent of the first day trip organised by Thomas Cook on 5th July 1841, when an excited party of Friends of Temperance travelled from the Midland Counties railway station in Campbell Street, Leicester, to Loughborough Central. The excursion cost 1 shilling each including transport via steam train, a cup of tea, a bun and musical entertainment from a brass band. This was the world's first package tour, from which the modern tourist industry developed. Leicester might well be called 'the birthplace of tourism', for the great travel firm of Thomas Cook & Son began here.

Thomas died in 1892 and his tombstone can be seen in Welford Road Cemetery, Leicester. His statue is outside London Road station (*inset*) and there are many other buildings and places associated with him in both the city and county; they are listed in *1841–1991: The Thomas Cook Trails* (Leicester Tourist Information Centre).

Barrow upon Soar

The river Soar flows diagonally through Leicestershire and divides it into two distinct parts. The river meanders in a wide floodplain, even now susceptible to frequent floods which cut off villages on either side from each other. Below Leicester twin villages face each other, mostly safe on their river terraces above the floodplain: Rothley and Cossington; Mountsorrel and Sileby; Quorn and Barrow upon Soar. The river itself has locks and weirs which half tame it, and in many areas large lakes are a reminder of the extensive gravel extraction in the valley.

By 1788 Loughborough had become an inland port following the canalisation of the Soar. Despite much opposition from coal-owners in west Leicestershire, the canal was continued to Leicester by 1794. The Grand Design linking the Thames–Trent–Humber via canal was finally achieved in 1814 and Leicester was the pivot.

Villages such as Barrow suddenly had wharves. Lime and other goods could be shipped out. Materials, including Welsh slates and bricks, could come in. Canal inns sprouted up, often with names such as Navigation Inn or Boat Inn. Street names reflected canal mania and in some places new suburbs were built near the canal.

Barrow had been important from early times. A prehistoric trackway known as the Salt Way ran from Belvoir near the Sewstern Way to Six Hills (later on the Fosse Way), to Barrow, then across the Soar to Beacon Hill, Charnwood, and beyond.

The lower Lias limestones found at Barrow produced lime which was famous regionally and further afield. Some buildings in the village still show evidence of its usage. In 1851 a plesiosaurus fossil in an excellent state of preservation was found in Barrow Lime Quarries, which are famous for reptile and fish fauna. On a roundabout known as Jerusalem in the village a stone replica can be found (*inset*) which has become the symbol of the place.

The old walls of Barrow also reflect the interesting, even remarkable geological background of the area. Many contain granite from Mountsorrel, over the river; boulders from the river bed; slate from Swithland; ironstone; limestone; fossils; and 18th-century bricks. Sometimes the buildings themselves have the same wealth of materials. It seems fitting to discover in the churchyard the grave of John Crossley, the man responsible for the 72¼-mile Settle & Carlisle railway (1876); one of the outstanding engineering feats of the 19th century, it was pioneered through hideously difficult geological terrain in the Pennines.

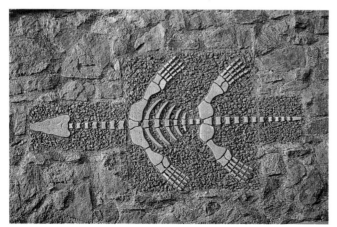

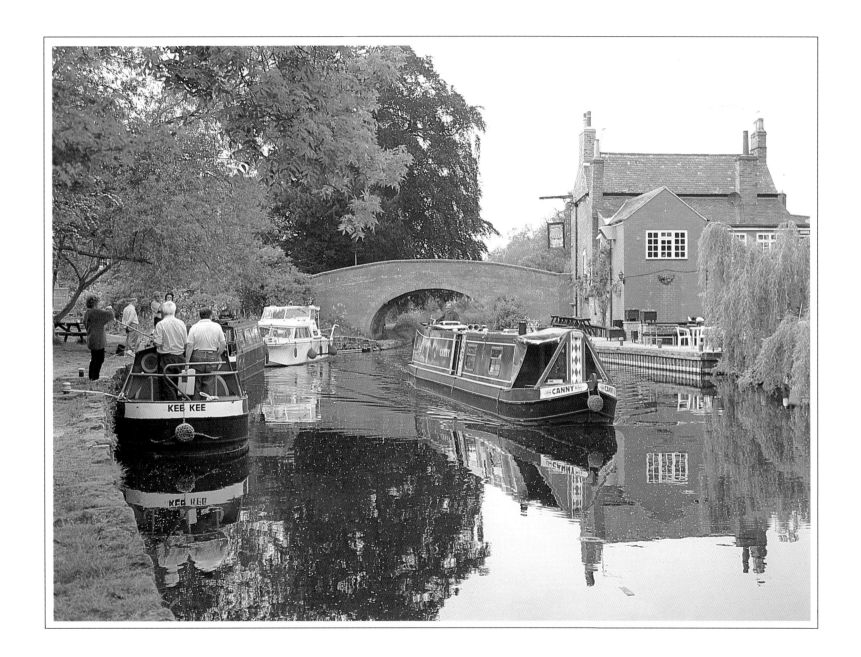

Foxton Locks

Foxton Locks were constructed on the advice of the great engineer Thomas Telford. A miracle of 19th-century engineering, they are joined at Bottom Lock by a branch canal from Market Harborough opened in 1809. When the link was finally made into Northamptonshire and the Grand Union Canal at Long Buckby, a daily service could be offered to 'all parts of England'.

The intricacies of supplying water to the canal system alone deserve special study, but, as with so many technological innovations, no sooner was the scheme completed than economic demands required improvements. Since it took at least one hour to navigate the staircase of locks, a quicker alternative was devised, namely an inclined plane at the side. This was opened in 1900 but because of insufficient traffic it was superseded and dismantled in 1911.

Recent and continuing restoration and conservation work have made the entire lock system a very fine sight and the inclined plane has also been cleared so that the visitor can inspect it closely. The former engine house is now a museum. It is particularly rewarding to look for small details such as signs, nameplates, old machinery and the artforms associated with the great canal era.

There are trails alongside the flight of ten locks and boats can be hired for canal trips. A short walk of ½-mile takes you to the village of Foxton, with St Andrew's church on the nearby hill and a famous swingbridge which is turned for barges passing along the canal. A strong Puritan centre, Foxton has a Baptist church dating from 1716 and an old court house near the small green.

Market Harborough is a few miles south-east of Foxton

Locks. It is one of Leicestershire's finest towns with the church of St Dionysius dominating the centre. Around the church, built about 1300, is the market place, part of the new town created at a crossing point of the river Welland in the late 12th century.

The main street has lovely Georgian houses along each side, with older buildings such as the Three Swans, a 16th-century coaching inn, and the Angel Hotel, which had stabling for 90 horses and 26 coaches per day passing through. A recent bypass has restored peace to the town.

The Old Grammar School (*inset*) was built by Robert Smythe in 1614 on stilts over the butter cross, in order to avoid controversy with tradesmen fearful of losing their stalls below. Even the town hall of 1788 had to be built on an upper floor, with shops beneath for the traders.

Such was the business zeal of shopkeepers in the past; today Market Harborough remains a lively, strategically placed town which is pleasant to live in.

Burrough Hill and Stilton Cheese

One of the best views in Leicestershire is from the Iron Age hill fort at Burrough Hill in the east of the county. Here, from a height of almost 700 feet, you can see in the distance Charnwood Forest and Leicester city to the west, Melton Mowbray to the north and Billesdon Coplow to the south. Nearer, you can see the village of Burrough on the Hill with its 13th-century church and marlstone buildings. Thickets of gorse and elder cover the slopes, and Burrough Hill covert has survived as a reserve for game birds and foxes, becoming well known as the border between the Quorn and Cottesmore hunts.

The earthworks are impressive. Hill forts were defensive camps and the ramparts would be surmounted by a timber palisade. Strong gates controlled the entry and in times of trouble livestock would be driven inside. Outside the ramparts was a deep ditch, the line of which can still be seen.

There has been some archaeological excavation at the site and pottery fragments and coins indicate that the fort was constructed about 2,100 years ago. It remained occupied for about 600 years. *Leland's Itinerary* (1540) records that at Whitsuntide people came to 'shoot, run, wrestle, dance and use other feats of exercise'. In the 1800s there were horse races here, probably inside the ramparts, with spectators gathered around. Today visitors come to fly model planes and kites and to picnic where once their ancestors eked out a difficult existence.

One mile south-east of Burrough Hill is the village of Somerby. Here, the Stilton Cheese Inn advertises the presence of this unique commodity (*inset*). As Trevor Hickman explains in his *History of Stilton Cheese* (1995): 'Somerby gained a reputation as a centre for Stilton cheese between the First and Second World Wars because of the excellent cheese made by Bill Fryer' of Grange Farm; the bulk of the produce was sold to Brasenose College, Oxford, the owners of the farm.

Stilton cheese became famous because a Mrs Frances Pawlett of Wymondham, Leicestershire, has been credited with its invention and its marketing at the Bell Inn, Stilton, on the Great North Road, owned by Cooper Thornhill. However, it appears that the first recorded reference to Stilton was made in 1722, when Mrs Pawlett was only two years old.

It is likely that, although Wymondham had a long history of cheese production, farmers' wives in other villages such as Braunston, Withcote and Little Dalby and at Quenby Hall were also making a similar cheese, often with a different name such as Slipcote or Berriffe's cheese. Mrs Pawlett and Cooper Thornhill, however, made it famous and the industry reached its heights in the early 19th century.

The 'king of cheeses' is predominant amongst Leicestershire's famous range of gourmet foods which includes Red Leicester cheese, pork pies and Melton hunt cakes.

Belvoir Castle

Belvoir Castle commands a wonderful view over several counties and it is a landmark from far away. The Norman name, meaning 'beautiful view', indicates its origins: the first castle on this site was built by Robert de Todeni, standard bearer to William the Conqueror, in the 11th century. Destruction by civil wars in the 15th and 17th centuries as well as a devastating fire in 1816 left very little of the original buildings and so the present castle dates from 1800–30.

There are numerous treasures in the castle, ranging from the gigantic elk's head dug out of an Irish bog and the bugle which sounded the Charge of the Light Brigade, to the hand-painted silks of the China Room, the painted ceilings, tapestries, busts and the famous picture gallery. The castle is the home of the 17/21st Lancers Museum. Outside, the gardens and grounds are outstanding.

Below the castle is the Vale of Belvoir, through which run the river Devon and the disused Grantham Canal. There are lovely villages located below the scarp from Long Clawson to Redmile and Bottesford. The Jubilee Way, a long-distance footpath, was opened in 1977 and extends from Melton Mowbray northwards along the scarp then down into the vale below Belvoir Castle, eventually turning east to join the Viking Way near Woolsthorpe, Lincolnshire.

Bottesford (*inset*) has many claims to fame. The stately spire of the church of St Mary the Virgin is a landmark for miles around and is known as the 'Lady of the Vale'. This is one of England's largest village churches and one of the best proportioned. The unrivalled series of tombs of lords of Belvoir Castle allows you to see eight earls, including six Knights of the Garter, at one time and in one place.

The church possesses a most unusual tomb recording the death by witchcraft of two heirs to an earldom. In the early 1600s, one Joan Flower of Bottesford cursed the 6th Earl of Rutland and all his family, which apparently resulted in the death of his sons and much illness. The inscription reads: 'two sonnes, both who dyed in their infancy by wicked practice and sorcerye'. This event led to the trial and execution of the Belvoir witches in March 1619.

The Codyngton brass (1404) is one of the finest of its kind in England, in particular because of the rich carving of the vestments of Henry de Codyngton, rector of Bottesford who died in 1404.

Bottesford has the distinction of being officially recognised as the last place to be attacked by enemy aircraft in World War Two – but no damage was done.

The Hunt

Whatever your opinion of fox-hunting, it cannot be denied that it has been a spectacular part of the rural scene in England for centuries. The traditional Boxing Day meet at Cutts Close in Oakham, Rutland, attracts over 2,000 people each year.

Leicestershire and the English Shires are at the heart of fox-hunting. Famous hunts such as the Belvoir (*opposite*), the Cottesmore, the Quorn and the Fernie are located in this area; indeed Billesdon Coplow, a local landmark and a focal point for the hunt, is immortalised in a poem, '*The Coplow Run*', which begins:

> With the wind at north-east forbiddingly keen,
> The Coplow of Billesdon ne'er witnessed, I ween,
> Two hundred such horses and men at a burst,
> All determined to ride, each resolved to be first,
> But to get a good start, over-eager and jealous,
> Two-thirds, at the least, of these very fine fellows,
> So crowded, and hustled, and jostled, and cross'd,
> That they rode the wrong way, and at starting were lost.

The fox features not only in the medieval carved capitals of several local churches but on many a weather vane in the area. It is on the Leicestershire coat-of-arms and is the emblem of Leicestershire County Cricket Club and Leicester City Football Club.

The landscape enshrines fox-hunting just as much in its coverts, fields and hedges, carefully conserved over many years to assist the hunter. Some coverts, like Botany Bay, can be dated by their names, in this instance the 1790s. Others may be named in memory of a huntsman, such as the covert planted near Owston in May 1974 in memory of Mr Gossage, secretary of the Cottesmore, who died in a hunting accident in 1970. One of the oldest coverts is Ashby Pastures in Quorn territory.

Melton Mowbray was much influenced by hunting; indeed the Belvoir, Cottesmore and Quorn meet in its market place. It was here that the Marquis of Waterford and his cronies 'painted the town red'. It became the hunting metropolis.

The Cottesmore is one of the oldest hunts in England and it covers much of Rutland. Tom Noel, an early master, wrote one of the first books ever published on the subject in 1732. His hunting diary is kept in Rutland County Museum. His hounds gained a great reputation for showing sport, retaining their fame ever since through notable masters such as the Yellow Earl, Lord Lonsdale. The Duke of Windsor (as he later became) frequented the area in the 1930s and now the Prince of Wales is often seen at one or other of the hunts.

The Fosse Way

The Fosse Way was constructed about 45 AD and ran from Lincoln to Leicester, then on to Bath and Exeter. It was virtually straight for 200 miles. In Leicestershire, the best-preserved section is a 4-mile stretch from High Cross to Stoney Bridge, near Sapcote.

At one time the Fosse Way marked the frontier of Roman Britain. It rises gently to High Cross on Watling Street, the important Roman road running from London to Chester. High Cross was a nationally significant road junction. A pillar was erected in 1712 to mark the centre of Roman England and the county council have plans to enhance or replace the monument in the future.

High Cross stands at 443 feet above sea level and the area is one of England's major watersheds, with streams such as the Swift and Avon flowing to the Severn, the Welland flowing to the Wash, and the Soar northwards to the Trent.

At one time near this junction there was a military

township and market centre called Venonis. Now the M1, M69 and M6 motorways surround the area and prove what good judges the Romans were as civil engineers. However, if you walk along the old Fosse Way in the heart of south-west Leicestershire you will find pleasant seclusion.

'The English landscape itself, to those who know how to read it aright, is the richest historical record we possess. There are discoveries to be made in it for which no written documents exist, or have ever existed'. The Fosse Way exemplifies the words of W. G. Hoskins so well. The many deserted villages of Leicestershire, over 70, also remind us of the same theme. They can be found all over the county, all over the Midlands, and all over Britain.

They are recognisable by the ridge and furrow of medieval fields preserved in the pastureland; by regular humps and bumps which represent the foundations of village houses; by old green ways; by the remains of fishponds and dams; by hollow ways worn down by centuries of usage; and, maybe, by a church standing lonely in a field with no village nearby.

Many of these clues can be found at Ingarsby (*inset*) in east Leicestershire. Hidden away in rolling countryside with sheep grazing where men, women and children once lived and loved, all that now remains is Ingarsby Old Hall.

Leicester Abbey depopulated this village in 1469 to enclose the fields and turn it into a sheep and cattle ranch ... much cheaper to run and more profitable. The Old Hall may have been the grange which administered the property. And so, in the words of the old chronicler, Walter Map, 'grass grows now where Troy town once stood'.

RAF Cottesmore

During the past 20 years the skies over Rutland have become more interesting than ever before. Rutland Water, opened in 1976, is a major international wildfowl sanctuary. Both the European Community and the World Wide Ramsar Convention have recognised its importance. More than 240 different species of birds have been attracted, some travelling up to 6,000 miles to reach the reservoir.

There are also unrivalled sunrises and sunsets over the water. Throughout its history Rutland lacked significant streams and waterways; now it has a large 'inland sea' and the sky has become more beautiful and dramatic.

An alien in the sky is the Tornado strike/attack aircraft based at RAF Cottesmore. As yet there seems to be no major conflict between birds and machines, but precautions have been taken from time to time. Continually, it seems to local inhabitants in Oakham and around, there are darting Tornados in the sky both day and night.

The Tornado arrived in 1980 and the Tri-National Tornado Training Establishment was formally opened at RAF Cottesmore in 1981. The first crews from Italy, Germany and Britain also arrived. More than 2,500 aircrew have been trained, and many, after a tour of duty with their national squadrons, have returned to Cottesmore as instructors. By 1999 this function will cease and RAF Cottesmore may no longer be the home of the Tornado.

From 1943 to 1945 RAF Cottesmore was under the control of the US Army Air Force, operating in a troop-carrying role. It was from here that paratroopers of the 82nd Airborne Division went to war: 'On 17th September 1944 Sunday morning worshippers on their way to church could hear the distant rumble of aero engines. On the airfield the biggest armada of aircraft yet seen in Rutland moved out of their dispersals and rolled towards the take off point like so many disciplined bees.'

Past, present and future, the sky forms Rutland's third dimension, and more than ever before, natural and man-made phenomena combine to enhance the scene.

Seaton Viaduct

On a misty morning in the Welland valley or in the dim twilight of a sultry summer's eventide you may receive a sudden surprise. Surely that isn't a Roman aqueduct across the valley? We know Rutland is remarkable, but can it really compare with Nîmes?

Yet, as you draw nearer, you can certainly discern something of a minor wonder. From Harringworth towards Seaton for ¾ mile with 82 arches each 70 feet high there extends a brick-built railway viaduct which, in its time, must have ranked as an engineering miracle.

Built between 1876 and 1878, it carried the LMS Kettering to Manton branch line and represents the peak of railway achievement in the area. Who would believe that a man-made object could do so much to enhance the pastoral Welland valley?

Years ago the 'Robin Hood Express' travelled this line from Nottingham to St Pancras, stopping only at the insignificant Manton station to pick up the odd prime minister or aristocrat who had spent the weekend hunting in the area.

Long Lyddington is within sight of the Seaton viaduct. The village has many lovely stone buildings, usually of rich brown ironstone. There are mysteries. Was the green really where we find it today? Was it bigger? Why is the village so long? Could it be to do with gradual reclamation of wetlands in the south? What mysterious part do Prestley Hill and Bee Hill perform in village history? Once, legend says, there was a maze on one of the hills.

Lyddington lost the battle with nearby Uppingham in medieval times to become the main market town, but it was important as the centre for the bishops of Lincoln until the 1500s. So large was the Lincoln diocese that visiting bishops had to have accommodation provided. The present Bede House (*inset*), newly restored, was the bishop's palace.

There is a fine hall with an exquisite 400-year-old ceiling of panelled oak with rich carving, heraldic glass, splendid fireplaces and richly moulded doorways. Outside, a precinct wall, with a tower known as the Bishop's Eye, surrounds a lovely garden.

The palace was turned into an almshouse in 1602. Next to it is St Andrew's church, and the two must comprise one of the most attractive conjunctions of buildings in the country. In the church are two excellent brasses, acoustic jars, and a Puritan arrangement of the four-sided communion rail. English Heritage now owns Bede House, which is open to the public.

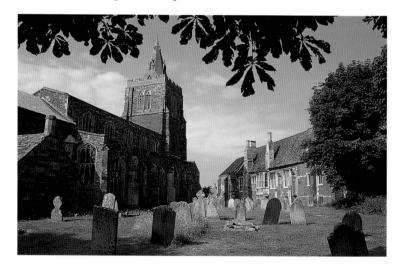

Uppingham

In the graveyard at Uppingham there is a chapel-like building which is the Old School founded in 1584 by Archdeacon Robert Johnson. A similar building can be found in Oakham churchyard, also founded in 1584 by the same man. These two modest buildings mark the beginning of two of England's great public schools – Uppingham and Oakham. They are still using the Old Schools today.

As in Oakham, church, school and market place lie very close together. There is a similar long High Street with back lanes and interconnecting alleys. However, whilst Oakham lies on flat ground, Uppingham is situated on a prominent ridge, so that viewed from the south it seems arranged along it. Though smaller than Oakham, it would make a fine county town. In fact, it lies along more important routeways, like the A47 linking Leicester and Peterborough.

Uppingham School occupies a good deal of the town along High Street West. Here the Victoria Tower (*inset*) provides the main entrance to the school. There is a statue of Archdeacon Johnson in a niche, holding a model of the original school. The tower was built between 1894 and 1897 by Sir Thomas Jackson, who did much to convey the atmosphere of a Cambridge college to the school buildings. The courtyards beyond and inside the tower gateway are redolent of this. Near this area a fine statue of the most famous headmaster of all, Edward Thring, presides over the day-to-day activities of the school. When he came in 1853 there were 25 boys, but by 1863 there were 200 and two years later 300. Today there are well over 700 boys and girls, including a junior school.

The County of Rutland

Even though Rutland was swallowed up by Leicestershire in 1974 county signs were retained on every entrance to the former county. There was a strong sense of local patriotism even though most of the population did not originate in Rutland. Most never doubted that the little county would one day regain its status, as it did in April 1997.

So precious was Rutland's status that, in 1973, the signs near Braunston were altered by a patriot so that they read: *Rutland – Rat Race Ends Here.* This sentiment had been inspired by the words of the great landscape historian W. G. Hoskins: 'One would like to think that one day soon at each entrance to this little county, beside a glancing willow-fringed stream, there will stand a notice saying *Human Conservancy: Abandon the Rat-Race at This Point.'*

Certainly Rutland seemed to be a rural haven. Only 17 miles across, its borders were well defined: to the south, the river Welland; to the east, the Fens; to the north and west, rising land. In the west too was the Royal Forest of Leighfield which merged into Rockingham Forest, and these woodlands marked the frontier. Hedge analysis has shown that some of the boundary hedges here are between 800 and 1,000 years old.

Place-names along the western frontier suggest that by the 6th century it was an ancient divide. Flitteris, near

Braunston; Twitch Hill, Ridlington; Wardley and Thunor Wood, Beaumont Chase; all indicate disputed areas, boundaries, look-outs, beacons and heathen cult sites (often located near boundaries).

Historians today believe that Rutland was a personal estate with well-marked boundaries over 1,500 years ago, and then became a royal estate before being established as a county in 1208.

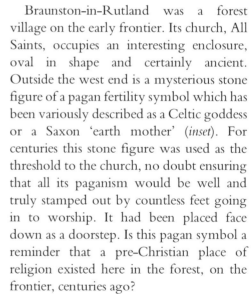

Braunston-in-Rutland was a forest village on the early frontier. Its church, All Saints, occupies an interesting enclosure, oval in shape and certainly ancient. Outside the west end is a mysterious stone figure of a pagan fertility symbol which has been variously described as a Celtic goddess or a Saxon 'earth mother' (*inset*). For centuries this stone figure was used as the threshold to the church, no doubt ensuring that all its paganism would be well and truly stamped out by countless feet going in to worship. It had been placed face down as a doorstep. Is this pagan symbol a reminder that a pre-Christian place of religion existed here in the forest, on the frontier, centuries ago?

Rutland's territorial uniqueness and its secret qualities make it quintessentially suitable to become a 'Human Conservancy … protected against incessant noise, speed and all the other acids of modernity'. Maybe one day it will find its true role.

Oakham Castle

Oakham is back again as the county town of Rutland, from April 1997 – although no true Rutlander ever thought it had ceased to be. The historical continuity reaching from as far back as 1208, when Rutland was recognised as a county, has been reaffirmed.

This vintage English market town with its classic combination of castle, market place, butter cross and stocks, with an old and famous school in close association with a magnificent church, is idyllic.

What you see today is the great hall of a fortified manor house, built by Walkelin de Ferrers, a leading Norman

knight, between 1180 and 1190. There was a previous hall here, recorded in the Domesday Book in 1086 as being worth two ploughs.

The castle is recognised as one of the finest examples of domestic Norman architecture in England and is the earliest surviving example of an aisled stone hall in the country. The gateway is 13th-century in style, but it was actually rebuilt in the 17th century by George Villiers, later Duke of Buckingham, who became lord of the manor in 1621. It matches similar gateways at his home, Burley on the Hill. The wrought-iron gates were added in 1872, replacing wooden doors. Decorative horseshoes and shields on the iron gates are a reminder of the real horseshoes which were nailed to the old wooden doors but later moved inside the castle (*inset*).

Inside the castle there is a surprise – a court room whose walls are covered with over 200 horseshoes. Magistrates and occasional crown courts are still held in the castle. Assize courts, with all their pageantry, were formerly held here. The horseshoes are forfeits paid by peers of the realm and royalty on journeys through Oakham over the centuries.

The tradition of demanding a horseshoe was first mentioned in writing in 1521, but it is said to date back to the 12th century. It was brought to Rutland by the Ferrers family of Normandy. The horseshoe is the heraldic emblem of this family and of Rutland too.

Some horseshoes are huge – the more important the person, the larger the horseshoe. They became symbolic and so there are not so many of the normal size; those that remain may be the oldest in the castle, but many have been lost or even stolen as trophies.

Burley on the Hill

Burley sits high on the scarp above the Vale of Catmose. Its name means 'fort in the clearing' and certainly the site is impressive. The little village was once a flourishing town with a yearly fair, but in 1375 it was destroyed by fire. The smithy (*inset*) has been restored. Though small, it is famous as the supposed inspiration for Longfellow's poem 'The Village Blacksmith'.

> Under the spreading chestnut tree
> The village smithy stands

The scene seems right and perhaps Longfellow attended the church just down the lane, Holy Cross, next to Burley on the Hill House.

The mansion at Burley attracts attention from all quarters and has been much enhanced by the creation of Rutland Water. The present house built by Daniel Finch, 2nd Earl of Nottingham, between 1694 and 1708 has inspired eulogies from the Rutland historian James Wright who described it as a 'Heaven-like-Palace' and from Macaulay, who admitted it was 'one of the noblest terraces in the Island'. A hundred years later Sir Nikolaus Pevsner echoed these sentiments: 'Many a ruler of a minor state in Germany would have been proud of such a palace.'

Burley House symbolises more than 2,000 years of continuity of settlement and although archaeological evidence is yet to be found, it is likely that an Iron Age hill fort was located there and that at a later period settlers moved down into the Vale of Catmose.

By the 15th century Burley had been acquired by the Haringtons of Exton. It was in this first large house in 1595/6 that lavish Christmas festivities included a performance of *Titus Andronicus* in which the London company of actors probably featured William Shakespeare.

During the Civil War the house was virtually destroyed by fire. It was acquired by the Finch family and rebuilt in 1694. The magnificent Doric colonnade exending 200 feet along the north front was based on that at St Peter's in Rome and provides one of the greatest surprises in Rutland. On the lawns nearby some of the first important cricket matches were played in the 1790s; they were introduced by George Finch, 9th Earl of Winchilsea, who was founder of the MCC. His servant, Thomas Lord, gave his name to the famous cricket ground Lords.

Burley was sold by the Hanbury family recently and has been tastefully converted to private residential accommodation.

Barrowden and Morcott Windmill

The village pond has disappeared from many parts of the English scene. Yet here in Barrowden the old duck pond, with the stone-built Exeter Arms nearby, provides that idyllic view so rare today. Rutland is very short of village ponds: so many have been filled in, deemed no longer necessary. In the past these watering places for animals were also used as sheep washes, and wooden wagon wheels could be swollen in them to prevent drying out in hot weather.

Barrowden has an ancient name, probably meaning burials on a hill. There has been a settlement here for centuries, covering the crossing point over the river Welland to the twin village of Wakerley. Located on Rutland's southern frontier, Barrowden was an important strategic settlement. Since the Welland is thought to have been one of the main routes of entry for invading Saxons and Scandinavians it was well placed, especially as it sits well above flood levels.

The large village green is the centre of a sizeable village today, with modern developments blending in well with the older stone cottages with their thatched or Colleyweston tile roofs. We are close to the great building-stone areas at Ketton, Clipsham and Barnack which provided the raw material not only for country cottages but also for cathedrals and other national buildings.

The walk to St Peter's church past Pepperday Cottage is a marvellous little ramble, the trees, walls and hedges enhancing the way. The high 14th-century broach spire is a landmark. Inside, at the patronal festival, rushes are strewn on the floor. Watch out for glow-worms. Barrowden is famous for them, though it likes to keep it a secret.

Once Barrowden was a royal manor with a weekly market and annual fair. Now, the closeness to the A1 means that the village is populated by commuters rather than farmers and labourers; but this is so with most of Rutland's villages.

Dominating the skyline a short distance away from Barrowden is Morcott windmill (*inset*), restored in recent years but not open to the public. Situated on a high ridge at over 300 feet, it is well placed for work – if any existed. Although those days are gone and the windmill is now converted to residential use, it still acts as a nostalgic reminder of the past.

Rutland Water

A church stands lonely on the southern shore of Rutland Water. From a distance it appears like a ship moored alongside a pier. As you approach it seems half hidden, as if being refitted in a dry dock. Apart from the great expanse of water there is little else around, except for a few buildings in a nearby wood.

As you walk along the shore, the church takes on different aspects, and it is best of all when silhouetted against the setting sun. On a sunny day, even from a distance, its stone shines out as a landmark.

Yet there is something odd about the church. It is unlike any other in rural Rutland; indeed, it looks like a city church. Its urbane modernity seems to defy the local tradition of rich-brown, rugged marlstone with squat and sturdy tower or ascending spire.

As you come closer to peep through the windows you will find no altar, no congregation or place for them, no organ music. Indeed, the church has been filled up inside so that the floor almost reaches the arches and the windows. No bells will ring from this sad church.

Once this was part of the great estate of the Earl of Ancaster. His house, Normanton Park, was demolished in 1926. All that remains are the stables, now the Normanton Park Hotel. The village of Normanton was depopulated about 1764. When Rutland Water was created in 1976 the church was saved on its protected causeway and it is now a Water Museum. Its tower and portico were built in 1826 and the nave in 1911, but the site is much older.

Now one of Britain's largest man-made lakes covers much of the old estate, leaving Normanton Tower as a solitary reminder of the strength of historical continuity.

A few miles away is Wing treatment works, which purifies the water from Rutland Water before it is distributed all over the surrounding area. Opposite one of the largest treatment works in Britain is Wing Maze – ancient and modern face each other across a country lane (*inset*).

This is a turf maze, one of very few in Britain. Its origin is obscure but its pattern preserves that of the Cretan labyrinth shown on Greek coins of the period. Is it a device to defeat the Devil? A form of penance? Was a maze dance associated with the foundation of the settlement? Is it a symbol of the human brain or life in the womb? Why should it be located in Wing? This is one of the few villages of Scandinavian origin in Rutland and there are many stone mazes in Sweden, where they are called *Trojeborg* (Troytowns), or *Steindanz* (stonedance) – could this be the explanation?

Tickencote

Three miles north of Stamford stands the wonderful late Norman church of Tickencote, 'embowered in trees, unknown to many and invisible to all those who pass by on the Great North Road' (now the A1). The *Church Guide* of 1936 has a moving introduction: 'The first impression one receives on standing before the marvellous chancel arch of six orders with the magnificent sex-partite vaulting behind is that of overwhelming awe . . . I know of no architectural work that has given me such a shock; it strikes one dumb with amazement.'

W. G. Hoskins wrote: 'No other region can show so many fine churches in such a small area', and John Betjeman added: 'Between 1150 and 1350 the villages of this area seem to have vied with each other as to which could build the finest church.'

Certainly St Peter's is of national importance. The chancel arch was built about 1130–50 and is most elaborate, with six carved rows that have different designs. The outer has square-cut foliage, the next chevrons, the third grotesques such as muzzled bears, a fox eating a monk's head, royal heads, cats' heads and monsters. The remaining rows are more restrained, with embattled mouldings, double zigzags, beak-head ornaments and plain round mouldings. H. V. Morton in his *In Search of England* writes: 'There is nothing that I am aware of like it in all England.'

The remarkable vaulting above the chancel dates from around 1160–70 and is also unique in this country, since it is thought that the style was not imported into England until 1175 by William de Sens for Canterbury Cathedral.

Such secrets may lie almost hidden in the tiniest village. Another surprise about Tickencote cannot be seen: its link with John Clare, the so-called peasant poet. John was born in Helpston, on the edge of the Fens, in 1793. For a time he worked at nearby Pickworth as a lime-burner. On Sundays, his only day off, he walked to Tickencote to have a drink in the Flower Pot, now much altered as Flower Pot Cottage.

One day, walking through the fields, he saw a pretty 18-year-old girl named Martha, daughter of William Turner of nearby Walkherd Farm. It was love at first sight and soon Clare became a frequent visitor to the farm. The couple were married in 1820, the year when his first book of poems was published. Martha was his inspiration and became his 'Sweet Patty of the Vale'.

John Clare expressed the serenity to be found at Tickencote when he wrote:

> There is a language wrote on earth and sky
> By God's own pen in silent majesty . . .
> And God's own language unto nature given
> Seemed universal as the light of heaven

Exton

Walkers coming into Exton from the Viking Way invariably head for the Fox and Hounds for a Ruddles County Ale to refresh them on their journey. The inn faces a lovely village green. Round about there are dream-like thatched cottages, creeper-covered walls, luxuriant gardens and odd street names such as Pudding Bag Lane. No wonder this village is so often chosen for film locations, as it was for *Little Lord Fauntleroy*.

Once, in the 12th century, King David of Scotland held lands here, and later Robert de Bruce. The Old Hall, near the church, now in ruins as a result of fire in 1810, was built by Sir James Harington in the reign of Elizabeth I. The New Hall was built in 1851 and has an imposing Roman Catholic chapel added to it. On this land the Noels, Earls of Gainsborough and Viscounts Campden, held sway. They still live here, and have had a great influence on the estate village over the centuries.

Exton Hall's great park was once a deer park, later turning into the attractive ornamental park of today with lakes, gardens and exotic trees. It is fitting that not far away, near the famous drive up to the Hall, Barnsdale Avenue, the late Geoff Hamilton's television gardens are located.

St Peter and St Paul's church is also in Exton Hall Park – or at least, like the village, on the fringes of it. As the humps and bumps near the church show, part of the village must have been around the church years ago, but now the church lies at a distance from the village.

The church is mainly 13th- and 14th-century, but was drastically rebuilt in 1850. It is imposing as you approach but its chief treasures are the fine monuments to the Noels and Haringtons inside. As Sir Nikolaus Pevsner wrote: 'There are no churches in Rutland, and few in England, in which English sculpture from the 16th to the 18th centuries can be studied so profitably and enjoyed as much as at Exton.'

Yet tranquil and idyllic as Exton may seem now, it is instructive to recall that only 25 years ago ironstone was quarried locally. In the 1950s United Steel opened up an untouched area at Exton, carefully taking the mineral line around the estate. This exploitation went on until 1973, when the giant dragline W1600 *Sundew* was removed from the area by being 'walked' to its graveyard at Harringworth 13 miles away. However, restoration of the land was so good that you have to look carefully to notice clues such as the slight depression of some fields below road level. Nearby, the Rutland Railway Museum is a reminder of days gone by.

The handwriting of history as recorded in the landscape reveals layer upon layer of the past in the Exton area. The recent discovery of the family papers of the Noels in the stables of Exton Hall is a major find both for Rutland and the nation. This large collection of documents is bound to illuminate past life and past landscapes – after all, there are about 600 boxes waiting to be read!

Melton Mowbray

Melton Mowbray has always been at the heart of a rich agricultural region famous for both cattle and crops as well as sheep and pig farming. This led to its development as a market centre as early as Domesday times; in fact Melton is the only Leicestershire market mentioned in the Domesday survey of 1086.

No wonder that two of Britain's most famous food products originate in this area – Stilton cheese, the 'king of cheeses', and the famous pork pie. Melton has been associated with pork-pie manufacture for over 150 years and they are still made in the traditional way today.

Cheese making gives rise to the byproduct whey, which is a good foodstuff for pigs – hence the two manufacturers of cheese and pork pies go hand-in-hand. Edward Adcock owned the first shop to sell pork pies in 1831 and his small shop in Leicester Street lasted until just before World War One.

Others were inspired to follow as demand grew. In 1840 Enoch Evans made pork pies in his baker's shop in Beast Market, now Sherrard Street, and by 1851 John Dickinson had rented a shop in Nottingham Street, to be joined by Joseph Morris in 1886. By 1901 this shop was known as Dickinson & Morris – now Ye Olde Pork Pie Shoppe – the oldest pork-pie bakery still left in town.

The popularity of Melton pork pies grew, particularly as the fox-hunt centred on the town found it convenient to take them out into the fields as a picnic. Enoch Evans set up the first pork-pie factory in 1860 at Thorpe End and was followed by Henry Collins and then in 1867 by Tebbutt & Crosher, and in 1928 by the well-known Tuxford & Tebbutt. By the 1870s the pork-pie industry

had reached its peak and it was written: 'Is not Melton Mowbray celebrated from the Indus to the Pole for its raised pies ... dispatched thousands of these delicacies everyday to all parts of the world by the morning passenger trains'. However, competition from all over the country led to a decline and the eventual closure of most of the factories.

You can see how to make a real Melton pork pie at demonstrations in Ye Olde Pork Pie Shoppe (*inset*). The Melton pie is special because it is baked without hoops or moulds for support. Also, the pastry is raised by hand round a pie block, then left to cool so that the lard firms up. It has bowed sides, not the straight sides found in copies. Best of all, if you call at the shop you will be able to taste free samples of the famous Melton pork pie on the counter.

The Wreake Valley

The river Wreake runs from beyond Melton Mowbray to join the river Soar, which then links with the mighty Trent. It is subject to flooding and in some parts, especially south of Asfordby, gravel quarrying has left large lakes, now sometimes used for recreation. A series of most interesting villages line each side of the valley, located well above flood levels. These form twin settlements, invariably opposite each other, as they stand in all their beauty on their own river terraces.

Hoby and Rotherby, Thrussington and Rearsby are such pairs. Nearby, Brooksby Agricultural College is

situated on the site of a deserted village, depopulated perhaps in the 14th century by the Black Death. The late 16th-century manor house and church remain, the former being the birthplace in 1592 of George Villiers, later Duke of Buckingham.

The headwaters of the Wreake begin east of Melton, partly in High Leicestershire and partly near Waltham on the Wolds and Buckminster. The oddity is that this stretch is known as the river Eye, but beyond Melton to the Soar it is called the Wreake, meaning in Old Norse 'twisted'. Certainly, the river Wreake does meander considerably below Melton.

Eye is an Old English name and it may well be that the headwaters of the stream were in an area of English settlement in the 9th century when the Danes arrived. The names Waltham, Buckminster and Wymondham suggest this. However, beyond Melton Danish names ending in '-by' proliferate and it seems likely that this was a major area of 'foreign' settlement.

The Domesday survey shows that in the 11th century the Wreake valley was one of the most highly populated areas in Leicestershire. It was also a leading agricultural region and has remained so ever since. The Wreake Navigation (the canal system opened in 1800), brought manufactured goods to Melton and took farming products to Leicester. In 1793 an Act of Parliament extended the navigable river to Oakham. The Oakham Canal was opened in 1802 but in 1846 the Syston–Peterborough railway destroyed any chances the canal trade had of prospering. Typical bridges of the time are still visible along the banks of the Wreake (*inset*) and the valley retains its exquisite rural charm.

High Leicestershire

Leicestershire is a county of contrasts. The valley of the river Soar divides it in two. To the west is the rugged hill country of Charnwood Forest, and beyond heavy clay lowlands where the National Forest is being created. To the east is High Leicestershire with a marlstone escarpment running diagonally across it, part of the Jurassic scarplands of England.

Here, many villages are sited on the glacial sand and gravel hills left long ago by the Ice Ages. Around them may be large areas of boulder clay, but on the scarp above the soils are rich brown and much lighter. For centuries this was a pastoral land and villages like Ingarsby were depopulated to become sheep ranches. It was force of necessity during World War Two that led to the 'dig for victory' policy which meant that so much pastureland became arable. Even today, much of the land remains arable, and fields of rape and flax can be seen.

There are mother and daughter settlements such as Hungerton – the 'hungry village' – with its daughters around: Baggrave, Ingarsby and Quenby. But the unrewarding soils and economic conditions led to the depopulation of these villages. The same fate befell Lowesby and Cold Newton. Close by is the 'town' of Hamilton which also disappeared, except for the earthworks in the fields.

This is the landscape of desertions – a lost landscape. There is even a 'lost' railway line running through it. Sometimes, as at Quenby Hall and Baggrave Hall, parkland has been created where villages once stood. Quenby Hall is one of the finest houses of its period (1620–30) in the county.

Gaddesby is one of the finest living villages in this area. As with so many settlements here, its Danish name-ending 'by' shows that this was a largely Danish-peopled district 1,000 years ago. The church and hall stand in close alliance. The former, St Luke's, 'is generally acknowledged to be the most beautiful village church in the county, both in its noble proportions and wealth of sculptured detail'. It was rebuilt between the end of the 13th and the beginning of the 14th centuries, being completed between 1340 and 1350.

The most famous monument in the church is that to Col. Edward Cheney at the battle of Waterloo, who had four horses killed under him and a fifth wounded within the space of 24 hours. Other battle scenes are depicted on the base of the statue. Only three statues similar to this are known to exist in English churches. However, it was not intended as a church monument and did not reach St Luke's until about 1917, when it was dragged on rollers from the Hall to the church (*inset*).

Hallaton

Hallaton is located in a beautiful part of east Leicestershire amidst plentiful streams, tiny valleys and a well-dissected landscape. The Welland valley is nearby and the old Roman road – the so-called Gartree Road – 2 miles away.

If you had to make an identikit picture of a typical English village it would surely be Hallaton with its duck pond, village green, butter cross, war memorial, motte and bailey castle site, rural vernacular buildings, small museum, school near the church, pubs with character and even its own folk custom of bottle-kicking on Easter Mondays.

Once, in medieval times, Hallaton was an important market town before Market Harborough emerged as its arch rival. In fact, the nearby village of Medbourne was also a competitor – perhaps that is how the bottle-kicking contest originated. Now the peaceful serenity all around belies the past.

W. G. Hoskins describes the castle as 'the finest example of a twelfth-century castle site in the county', with its large earth mound surrounded by a deep ditch flanked by a steep-sided valley and a stream. The castle protected an important industrial site where iron-working took place.

St Michael's church has a most imposing west tower with a broach spire of the 14th century and a fine octagonal pinnacle – a beautiful example 'that would take a place in the first rank of any county of England'. The view from across the fields stays in the memory for a long time.

The ceremony of the bottle-kicking takes place near the stream between Hallaton and Medbourne each Easter Monday. A huge hare pie is cut and distributed at the rectory in Hallaton, then a battle commences for the possession of two wooden bottles or casks which are filled with beer. Hundreds of people come from all over the county and even further afield to battle it out on Hare Pie Bank. This may be a pagan custom, it could have been associated with the demarcation of parish boundaries, or it may simply have been a game – perhaps one of the many forerunners of rugby?

This is excellent walking country, but with such heavy clay around you need stout boots. There are splendid views and enormous arable fields. History is all around and the landscape holds many secrets waiting to be discovered.

Kirby Muxloe Castle

William, first Lord Hastings, was one of the most powerful and wealthy men of his time. Besides receiving a large pension from the king of France, he held great offices and owned extensive estates. He had a private army that took an important part on the Yorkist side in the Wars of the Roses, which drew to a close in the 1480s.

He was 'one of the foremost builders of his time' and, in 1474, was given a royal licence to fortify three manor houses in Leicestershire and to create parks in each place. These were at Ashby-de-la-Zouch, Kirby Muxloe and Bagworth, all in the west of the county.

Little seems to have been done at Bagworth, which was described as a ruin by Leland in 1540. Building on a grand scale began immediately at Ashby castle and a few years later, in 1480, at Kirby. All three were amongst the last heavily fortified houses built in England.

Most of Leicestershire's outstanding and easily workable building stones are to be found in the east of the county, which is where the majority of its large houses were located. Bricks, used much by the Romans to build the Jewry Wall in Leicester, seemed to be the best option for Ashby and Kirby in the west. Kirby is one of the 'finest examples of medieval brickwork in the whole of England'. The bricks were made on site.

Lord Hastings enlarged and deepened the moat at Kirby and erected a massive tower commanding the drawbridge. It was intended to have brick towers at each corner of this beautifully symmetrical construction. However, in the summer of 1483, Lord Hastings was beheaded in London and work on the castle ceased the following year; it was never to be resumed, although the house was occupied by the Hastings family until the early 17th century. Now, the gatehouse is apparently used by the local policeman as his 'police station'.

The story of Kirby is linked to the denouement of the Wars of the Roses at the battle of Bosworth in August 1485. Richard III, who ordered the execution of Lord Hastings, was himself killed only 8 miles from Kirby on the fateful day that ushered in the Tudor dynasty.

The fate of Lord Hastings is mirrored by that of Samuel Adcock who 'fell by violence from the hand of an assassin' in 1854 as he was returning from Leicester one night. This is recorded on a tombstone in St Bartholomew's churchyard which ends with useful advice for both victims:

> Boast not thyself of tomorrow for thou
> Knowest not what a day may bring forth

Rothley and Mountsorrel

Rothley and Mountsorrel are located a few miles apart, on the flanks of scenic Charnwood Forest to the west and the floodplain of the river Soar to the east; yet they are very different villages in appearance and history.

Rothley, sitting above Rothley Brook, is more compact. The church of St Mary and St John the Baptist is a large and impressive building of local stone. The interior is mostly 14th-century, but the chancel was rebuilt in 1878 and the outside has also been heavily restored. There is a Saxon cross of the 9th century – one of the indications that Rothley was a minster in those times.

Many interesting monuments inside the church remember the Babington family, who owned the nearby house of Rothley Temple from 1565 to 1845. Anthony Babington plotted to kill Queen Elizabeth I and replace her with Mary Queen of Scots, for which both he and Mary were executed. More salubrious is Thomas Babington Macaulay, English historian, born at Rothley Temple in 1800, who 'introduced a new style into English literature ... exhibiting a power of picturesque narrative and a wealth of allusion which have never been surpassed'.

The village centres on Cross Green, but the original focus was Town Green. There are at least 11 cruck buildings of 16th-century date. A short distance away upstream lies Rothley Temple, now the Rothley Court Hotel. In 1203 the Knights Templar were granted land here which eventually passed to the Knights Hospitaller in 1312. The fine late 13th-century chapel remains and the rest of the house is an attractive mixture of medieval, Elizabethan and late Victorian styles.

Mountsorrel was a linear village, predominantly of local pink granite buildings and once industrialised. Its growth was compressed between the fine castle site, the river (canalised as the Grand Union) and the Leicester–Derby road, whose traffic is now thankfully deserting the village for the A6 by-pass in the river meadows. Mountsorrel is creeping towards Rothley via the so-called Rothley Plain. There are good views from Castle Hill.

Mountsorrel is a fascinating place, well worth walking around. The market cross (*inset*), a domed rotunda on eight Tuscan columns, was built in 1793 to replace the original cross taken by Sir John Danvers to Swithland Hall. There are several modern monuments in the village and the canal basin with its pretty bridge, lock and Waterside Inn, composes a memorable scene.

Market Bosworth

The city of Leicester is located centrally in the county. Within 20 miles a string of fine market towns surround the city – Melton Mowbray, Oakham, Market Harborough, Lutterworth, Market Bosworth, Ashby-de-la-Zouch and Loughborough. Though one of the smallest, Market Bosworth has a famous history and an attractive townscape.

Bosworth battlefield lies only 3 miles to the south and as you walk up Ambion Hill, the spire of St Peter's in Market Bosworth can be seen. The town has been drawn westwards towards the Ashby Canal and alongside this runs the vintage railway known as the Battlefield Line.

In the town today, at the right time of year, the magnificent floral displays set up for the 'Britain in Bloom' competition are an impressive sight and the busy market has a satisfying neatness and sense of enclosure. At first, many of the surrounding buildings appear to be 19th-century, but on closer inspection several are seen to be much older, with timber framing.

Dixie Grammar School (refounded in 1828) contrasts well with the curved line of lower buildings to the south-west. Particularly attractive are three 16th- and 17th-century cottages in the narrower part of the market. The Dixies bought the manor of Bosworth from Henry, Earl of Huntingdon, in 1567. By 1660 they were raised to the baronetage and early in the 18th century were rich enough to build Bosworth Hall, 'the best house of its period in Leicestershire'. The Hall has a fine south front and is situated on an earlier manor-house site. St Peter's church is close by the Hall and there is a lovely view to it up Church Street. The church was much rebuilt in the 14th century, with some remodelling in the 15th century.

Bosworth Park, once part of the Dixie estate, was bought by the county council in 1970 and is now a finely developed country park which adds greatly to the rural setting of Market Bosworth.

One of Market Bosworth's claims to fame is that Dr Samuel Johnson, born not so far away in Lichfield, started to teach at Dixie Grammar School about 1732. Apparently he had a very unhappy time, which is perhaps not surprising considering that 'he was a big, clumsy young man, his face was scarred by a disease he had when he was a boy and he jerked it about, grimacing and muttering in a way that sometimes terrified strangers'. Still, he was to become the most famous literary man of his day and his great *English Dictionary* was a masterpiece.

Stoke Golding

Stoke Golding is in south-west Leicestershire, near Hinckley. Watling Street lies to the south and a nameless Roman road to the north of the village. The line of a deserted railway runs close to the Ashby-de-la-Zouch Canal, which comes near to the village and enhances views of it. Northwards is the battlefield of Bosworth.

On Crown Hill, just outside the village to the west, Sir William Stanley placed the crown taken from Richard III on the head of the victor, Henry, Earl of Richmond – he became Henry VII.

To the north of the village is Daddington, and in the small 13th-century church of St James is a notice with another reminder about the battle: 'Henry VIII founded a chantry here for the souls of those killed at the Battle of Bosworth fought at Redmore in this parish. The bodies of many slain were brought here to be buried.'

St Margaret's church, Stoke Golding, is 'worth cycling twelve miles against the wind to visit!' according to John Betjeman. Hoskins agrees that it is 'one of the best churches in the Midlands ... its arcades would do credit to a cathedral in their beauty'. Pevsner adds that it is 'one of the most beautiful churches in Leicestershire, not large, but very grand and noble'. The church was built almost entirely in the reign of Edward I by Sir Robert de Campania and his wife Margaret.

The Ashby Canal was built between 1794 and 1804. It ran south for 30 miles at a height of 300 feet above sea level to join the Coventry Canal at Marston junction near Nuneaton, and it was lock-free except for the stop-lock at Marston. The intention had been to link with the river Trent to the north, but the canal never reached beyond Ashby Woulds near Moira. Here, by clever use of tramways, coal and other materials were transported to the canal and thence to southerly parts. Much of this traffic would pass Stoke Golding.

The Ashby Canal Company was bought out by the Midland Railway Company in 1845 but traffic still used the canal until the 1940s when, because of subsidence problems, the northern section had to be closed and eventually filled in. However, in recent years, much of the canal has been restored as a recreational and tourist route, since it links the former industrial landscapes of Moira and Swannington with Market Bosworth, Bosworth battlefield and Hinckley. The continued development of the Battlefield Railway next to the canal, with its interesting museum and locomotives at Shackerstone, adds to the appeal. The Ashby Boat Company runs three fully equipped traditional narrow boats from the Canal Wharf, Stoke Golding, which help to revive the atmosphere of the canal's heyday.

Stoney Cove and Twycross Zoo

An attractive leafy lane leads to an undistinguished building which sits below a towering quarry face. All around, the sides of the quarry seem to engulf the tiny cabin. In the centre of the quarry is a very deep lake, now the setting for the National Diving Centre and for watersports. The tiny building is a very popular public house called the Cove. From its balcony customers can sit in the sunshine and watch all the multifarious activities associated with diving.

Stoney Cove was once a thriving quarry known as Lane's Hill, which included Top Quarry and Stanton Top Pit. It extracted the valuable igneous rocks which also occur at other nearby locations such as Enderby, Narborough, Croft and Sapcote. Like many disused quarries in the area, its ultimate fate was flooding. Sometimes quarries become landfill sites, sometimes they are filled in and built on; mostly they remain in some form an identifiable part of the landscape.

Watersports of a different kind can be seen at Twycross Zoo, 15 miles north-west of Stoney Cove (*inset*). This has been one of Leicestershire's greatest attractions for many years. Molly Badham and her friend Nathalie Evans started with a pet shop in 1949, moved to a 'Chimps' bungalow in Hints, Warwickshire, but then, having developed an increasing passion for primates, came to Twycross, which was opened by TV star Jean Morton in May 1963.

Since then the animals have become famous for their appearances on television advertisements for Brooke Bond tea, and on many other occasions. The zoo serves two very important groups – visitors and the animals. The former have facilities for study, entertainment and wonder. For the animals it is a safe haven, where preservation, research and breeding programmes for threatened species can be carried out.

As long ago as 1979, Gerald Durrell wrote: 'Molly Badham's collection is one of the best in the British Isles. She has always had a tremendous rapport with her animals and has looked after their physical and mental well-being in a way that should be an example to some of the larger, established zoological gardens.'

History in the Landscape

The landscape historian W. G. Hoskins, wrote: 'The English landscape is, to those who know how to read it aright, the richest historical record we possess.' He knew and loved Leicestershire and Rutland landscapes better than most, and was especially fond of east Leicestershire and Rutland: 'It is a landscape on which, after so long an acquaintance, I look back with almost unclouded affection: ... where I first walked ... as a young man, ignorant of what I was looking at; ... returning from longer expeditions into microscopic Rutland, or the wonderful blue distances of Leicestershire.'

The landscape around Uppingham and Hallaton (*inset*) illustrates the depth of historical continuity to be found. Fields, hedges, walls, buildings, earthworks, boundaries, woods and many other features in the landscape are clues waiting for the vigilant observer to decipher. A study of the documentary records reveals even more discoveries, and the Ordnance Survey map itself is 'the handwriting of history', ready to disclose further secrets.

For example, Hoskins was able to identify Hallaton as part of a large estate belonging to a Danish noble, Toki, in 1066. He found evidence to suggest that the external boundary of the estate may have dated back to AD 1000; therefore, some hedges in the area may be over 1,000 years old.

Field patterns can still indicate the history of an area. Regular, larger fields may indicate 18th-century enclosures, and a more intricate, smaller pattern may represent much earlier enclosure from forest or wasteland. Perhaps a deer park may be discovered, as at Flitteris near Braunston-in-Rutland. A dead-end road or lane, as at Ridlington, may show how a great forest blocked the way, in this case the Forest of Leighfield.

Earthworks, alone in a field, may indicate a deserted medieval village, as at Ingarsby, Whatborough and Martinsthorpe. Here the landscape and its settlements have lived and died. Aristocratic houses or their remains and the creation of parkland are a striking feature of the landscape and the process of change is still going on. The great house at Normanton Park in Rutland has gone. On its site is Normanton Park Hotel. In its parkland lies Rutland Water.

So the landscape holds many secrets that still wait to be discovered. Like Professor Hoskins we may begin to explore it for pure pleasure, not really knowing what we are looking at, but eventually we realise that it poses problems which fieldwork, map, document or a conversation with locals may solve.

Beacon Hill

Beacon Hill is 818 feet high and is the second highest point in Leicestershire after Bardon Hill. The county council purchased the 213 acres comprising Beacon Hill from the Beaumanor estate in 1946. Now the hill can be approached by the public on all four sides. From the summit there are wonderful views over Loughborough and the Soar valley, even as far as the power stations in the Trent valley. On a clear day you may see Belvoir Castle on its scarp, Billesdon Coplow, and to the north the Derbyshire hills – some say that Lincoln Cathedral, 60 miles away, can be seen occasionally.

There is evidence that Beacon Hill was used in prehistoric times and, to some extent, the man-made contours on the slopes seem to indicate this. Because of its prominence, it is likely that an Iron Age hill fort was located here, similar to that at Burrough Hill in the east of the county.

A Bronze Age axe and hoard is the earliest discovery which gives some support to early settlement or use of the site. The hill is a scheduled ancient monument and it is an offence to damage it or to use a metal detector there. One day archaeological excavations may reveal more details about the role of Beacon Hill in the history of the Midlands.

The whole geological structure of the surrounding Charnwood Forest can be seen from the summit of Beacon Hill. A huge fold of rocks has been breached during the last 600 million years to leave a series of broken, horseshoe-shaped parallel ridges of which Beacon Hill, Broombriggs, the Brand and Swithland Woods form a part.

This ancient area of Pre-Cambrian rocks is one of the oldest in Britain and is surrounded by a plain composed of younger rocks. For many years it was thought that no fossils would ever be found in such ancient rocks until a schoolboy, Roger Mason, discovered the oldest fossil in the world in 1957. This was a fossil plant 700 million years old and it was named after him *Charnia masoni*.

On Beacon Hill itself, the crags can be seen to be striped in layers of green, grey and cream colours. Much of this is volcanic ash deposited in a sea. Several volcanic eruptions were involved and about 600 million years ago mountain-building tilted the rocks into their present craggy positions. Hardened volcanic dust and ash were split into very sharp protrusions called hornstones. Who could have believed that this beautiful area was once a group of island volcanoes in a wide ocean?